First published in Great Britain by
L.R. Price Publications Ltd., 2020.

This edition published by
L.R. Price Publications Ltd.,
27 Old Gloucester Street,
London, WC1N 3AX
www.lrpricepublications.com

ISBN: 9781838061029

Dedication

"To my amazing daughter who read my manuscript and gave me the courage to find a publisher."

Plenty of Flounders

*

Jo Roberts

1. A vacancy

"44-year old divorced, brunette teacher seeks a relationship.
Very loving and kind, although quite short in stature; enjoys travel, reading, cooking and spending time with her daughter...
Daughter is growing up now, and would like someone to take on the role of full-time companion for her mother.
If you would like to apply for the position, please message for further information."

Dating is a personal thing: what is right for one is not right for another.

This is the story of my successes and failures in the world of online dating, and the murky pond that it can sometimes be. Although written from a woman's perspective, my experiences are equally relevant to the male population, whom I am sure have found just as many problems, in their own search for a partner. It's a new world - one that it appears many of us now embrace, in our quest to find our life companion. Some of us are luckier than others. For a proportion, it is only a game; for me, it was a way of meeting my possible soulmate. I just never expected to find so many sprats along the way!

To date, I have entered the pond three times over a period of eight years. No, I'm not insane – although, following some of the messages I have received, I could well be heading that way! Three times might seem like a lot, but - and it is a *big* but - things don't always go according to plan.

My first experience came around ten years ago when, as a slightly more mature woman, with a teenage daughter, I found myself divorced - with very little confidence, a small amount of self-esteem and a lot of evenings to fill. Although I would head out with friends, the men I tended to meet locally didn't float my boat; there was nothing wrong with any of them, but their life goals and mine were vastly different: I didn't plan on frequenting the same pub, on the same days of the week, for the rest of my life - this seemed to be the intention of many.

A lot of the people I would have once hung out with were now married or in committed relationships and, although I like a bop, nightclubs weren't really an option, at this point in my life. I found myself at an age where my friends were all bringing up younger children, so doing anything as a group was becoming less of an option, too. Saturday nights were passing me by. Although I was happy in my life, it was missing the "coupley" side of things.

It was also starting to impinge upon my daughter's budding social life, as I had lots of time to monitor her activities!

Then, one day, enter the daughter's best friend, with the tale of a mum who had recently met a man through an online dating site, and was blissfully happy.

"Noooooooo way!!" said I.

An hour and a half later, I had a profile.

My experience began.

2. Do you have a type?

With my mini-bio live on the worldwide web, and a reasonable photo of myself - in which I looked human enough to bait the hook - I started my search.

I considered the type of man I was looking for and, other than the obvious (that they needed to be breathing!), I found that the pictures presenting themselves upon my search were varied. Delving further, I looked at the basic information and found that I was ruling out short, bald men – sorry guys, but you're obviously just not my type.

I had never considered that I had a type before, having dated blonds, brunettes and redheads in the past - yet, it appeared that when confronted with only the briefest of information, and a "bathroom shot", I had certain types that I would not consider. I'm short - *very* short - but for some reason, with no real idea why, I found that I was searching for someone over the five-foot-ten mark. Why I didn't find a man without hair attractive also posed a problem, as there was no reason not to. But, the daydream of running my fingers through his locks was one which I just didn't feel able to give up, so for me the appeal just wasn't there.

So, having set my search criteria, and a distance of fifty miles from my home address, I started reading in more depth.

As the days passed and I checked my inbox, I was delighted to see it filling up rapidly - wasn't I popular?! Unfortunately, it was filling with men whose profiles were a complete contrast to mine.

Pausing for thought, I started to realize that many hadn't actually read my carefully constructed bio; I could have written about having Hannibal Lecter-type tendencies, a need to spend their money and twenty children, yet they would still have messaged me.

I continued to look at the small photos, and tried to make my judgement calls on the variety of men which popped up.

3. A picture tells a thousand stories

There is an obvious problem with using a picture as a means of judging your "lifelong partner" to be. I don't like judging a book by its cover, nor a person on looks alone.

For me, this became a hurdle to overcome: I found that rather than looking at the person in the snap, I was considering the background of the photo, to give me tell-tale clues about the person.

So many pictures of bathrooms passed before my eyes, with men bearing their chests before the mirror. *Why not get a friend to take a proper picture?* I moved on from these.

I also completely ignored those who presented their manhood, in all its glory (the *way too much, too soon* bracket), also deciding against all of those holding a fish they had caught. I don't have anything against fish, but having a couple of anglers as friends, I was well aware of their wives' frustration at the long weekend absences, and didn't want to find myself in the same situation. Nor did I particularly want the smell of fish lingering around the house.

Am I really so fussy?

It appeared that I was.

I also found a dilemma over those with their children in the picture, partly because of my background in teaching and child protection, thanks to which I tended to see the web as an open door to some very unscrupulous characters. Also, partly because, in my mind, this was something that should be saved until you know someone a little better.

I knew that, practically, I didn't want to meet someone who had young children, having by now reached the stage that my daughter was self-sufficient; getting herself to school, finding the toaster and cleaning her room. Still, I also took the view that if a man was right for me, then children could fit into the equation; I didn't completely rule out the possibility.

Looking into the beautiful, brown eyes of one hopeful man, I found myself wondering how long his washing-up had been sitting there, as it appeared to take up the whole of the background. Another, with a cheeky grin, had an ironing board and a mountain of creased clothes behind him - I considered whether he was looking for a relationship, or a housekeeper. Shots of tall men, posing in orchards or by the sea, appealed far more.

There were, of course, the profiles which contained no photo at all, and it did make me wonder why they didn't want to show themselves. Still, having read a lovely profile of one man, sadly lacking a picture, I took a chance and messaged him. His response was good, and the messages went back and forth for a few days. When I finally asked for a picture, although he was sweet and obviously intelligent, I felt so sorry that having now seen him, I knew there was no way I would want to wake up next to him, every day, for the rest of my life. I'm sorry if that makes me appear shallow, but the lack of teeth and a huge wart just wasn't something I wanted to see on the pillow next to me, as I opened my eyes.

Crowd shots proved confusing: was I supposed to pick out the man to whom I thought the profile related, or was I intended to look at the whole group, and leave the details to my imagination? I decided to leave them alone as well.

This was also true of the close-up eye shot (!). Yep, nothing else but an eye - perhaps the advent of a Dalek invasion, I considered, as I added it to my *nope; not going to happen* list.

Then, the bunny ears and noses arrived!

It's bad enough that the social media sites have my lovely friends sprouting these app-generated accessories, and they are females; but, on a bloke…? *Noooooooo…*

So shallow and fussy!

Would I ever find someone who met my exacting standards, I wondered.

4. Selling yourself

Profiles are an interesting proposition. I had kept mine fairly short and sweet (no one needed to know my life story straight away, and I didn't think that anyone would want to know the negatives in my world), offering just enough to enable some sort of judgement on me. Because that is exactly what we are doing: with the simple press of a button, you are rejected and will probably never know it.

After having read through several-hundred male profiles, I adapted and changed mine, to see if it would generate further interest (bearing in mind the number which didn't even read them in the first place!).

Men's profiles proved to be varied and fascinating. Skipping past the ones which mentioned handcuffs, I pondered over one which told me that he was "V.W.E."...

Hmmmm...

Well, that gave me an opening line, to message what appeared to be a rather tall, good-looking man. His response (and my obviously naive knowledge of life) ruled him out immediately: for those of you as naive as myself, the acronym stood for "very well endowed".

Many profiles comprised of the sentence: "will fill this in later", or "just ask". I decided that if they hadn't bothered to write something, even small, then they might not be bothered to answer any messages. So, I moved on.

Disregarding men who listed their hobbies as fishing, golf and darts gave me a much shorter list to work through. I don't have any problems with these sports, but the thought of a man sitting on a cold riverbank, playing with his trout, or swinging a metal stick around whilst chasing a ball and a bogey; or, watching my beloved resting his pint on his stomach, whilst squealing out the immortal call *"one hundred and eiiigghhhtttyyyyyyyy!!"* didn't seem at all suited to my fairly sedate life and keenness to travel.

Quite a few said that they weren't writing much, as "no one reads profiles". This was not helpful to me, as I felt that the profiles were at least giving me some idea of the person, and any common interests we might have.

Gingerly dipping my toe into the water, I sent off a couple of messages to likely candidates and waited for the responses to come flooding in...

They didn't. I could see that men had viewed my profile, and got in touch, but the lack of a follow-up told me clearly that I wasn't for them. Being a polite sort of person, I decided that I would always send a reply (if I ever received a message, that was!), even if it was just to say sorry, that they weren't for me. The courteous approach isn't without its problems, though: much later in my search, one man who had received one of my sorry messages came back asking why he wasn't for me. This left me in something of a dilemma, because the courtesy angle of not wanting to leave something unanswered was in conflict with my most likely candid response: "Because I consider you to be short, bald and, having read your profile, very self-absorbed!"

*

By my third visit into the murky depths, my profile read along these lines:

> *"I travel... a lot!*
> *Looking for Mr. Right to join me!*
> *I'm an open book: ask and I shall always give you the truth; I have nothing to hide (the small pot belly being the exception!), love laughing, travelling (any country, at any time), cooking (you could always wash up!), reading (anything I can find on my Kindle), music (depends on the mood, but a huge range of stuff).*
> *I am independent and happy, but I miss being part of a couple and all that goes with it.*
> *Message me for more..."*

It offered an opening into my life, and would hopefully put off anyone who wasn't travel orientated.

The first message response to this profile came from a sweet gentleman, who revealed, after five messages, that he didn't think he would like travelling!!!

Over time, my profile changed, becoming shorter and shorter, at one point even including one which read:

> *"If you're breathing, please feel free to message!"*

Yes, I know I'm a hater of the one liner, but since no one seemed to be reading them anyway, what would it matter?

Surely, I couldn't be that desperate? But, after a few months of online dating, who knows?

5. Reading between the lines

With my growing interest in profiles, I started to read between the lines...

Following are a range of profiles I came across through the years. I have not altered the spelling or grammatical errors in any way, even though the teacher part of my soul was itching to do so!

MARK

"Okay, I'm sure you've read dozens of profiles, I guess most of which are pretty much the same, so I thought I would make mine a little different, hopefully you will smile, that's the intention. If it's naff, then please accept my opologies in advance, however if you do end up with a smile on your face, the why not send me a message. I will be getting Simon Cowell to help judge any replies, so if I don't get back to you it's because the miserable sod has hit the red button.

Oh, by the way, I don't have 'meet me' so pass over that option.......

*Well here goes.... My ***** poem. If you don't like it, no verbal abuse please. That said here goes nothing.....*

I may not be George Clooney, Johnny Depp, one even Mr Pitt,
however there's a resemblance to Forrest Gump, to that I will admit.
* *. *
I think of myself as funny, caring, warm and kind,

Chatty and articulate, strong in heart and mind.

..*

I don't need looking after, the washing machines a cinch,
I'm happy to share the cooking, I can do that at a pinch.

..*

I'm looking for my soulmate,to cherish when I hold.
A love to be more precious than a mountain made of gold.

..*

We could stand in bustling cities, with people rushing by,
And yet I notice no one, as I gaze into her eyes.

..*

I'm happy wearing flip flops, I scrub up in a suit,
My bum looks good in gym shorts, as well as jeans to boot.

..*

So, if you want a cheeky fella, with a twinkle in his eye,
Then you need not search no longer, maybe I'm your guy. ????

Okay, maybe it was a poor effort, but hey, at least I've made an effort.
Take care, Mark"

What a winning profile! It made me laugh, which is always a good start in my world. I thought about my response and, still chuckling quietly to myself, I messaged him...

Yep, no reply. What a shame.

MALCOLM

"Yes I AM single, No, I'm NOT married or in any relationship, there you go, we've got that out of the way now, so please read on :-)

How would I describe myself? Lol, surely its better for someone else to do that as long as its good? Well I do have a nutty sense of humour , love my music, love partying, love dancing, love socialising but not so much that I cant enjoy a nice evening in with the right company . I do take some pride in my appearance, I try to be fairly smart and well groomed when I can.

Cant say that I'm a book worm, I'm more in to my music - I like going out, but that doesn't happen very often with me being back to this area after being away for 8 years the people I knew had moved on or away.

I go to the gym but it's not something that I'd put before someone else but it gives me something constructive to do.
My ex was a 'lights off and quilt over us' type and I'm quite the opposite, so make of that what

you will :-)

I have a wicked an often warped sense of humour, which with talking to me you would get to see much more than this stuffy description of myself is making out that I have. I sometimes get called childish and will not deny that, I'll be a boring old fart when I feel the time is ready. I've nothing against doing the old 'cuddle up on the sofa with some wine and a dvd' routine as long as it isn't every night, that would get boring.

I'm fairly well travelled having been to Corfu, Rhodes, Zante, The Algarve, Tenerife, Gran Canaria, Tenerife, Lanzarote, Egypt (ugh), Prague, New York, Dubai, Singapore, Australia and Turkey

I don't mind cooking, I wouldn't say I'm very creative, but will try any recipe so I'd be happy to cook for the right person.

Relationships either work or they don't for the people involved, regardless of what form that relationship takes. So if you are a woman who analyses situations too much, who won't act reasonably, who takes trivial acts, magnifies them, and doesn't recognise romantic gestures, then let's not waste each other's time.

I didn't want to have to put this, because I don't like profiles that state more about what a person shouldn't be rather than the positives about themselves, but it seems to be a trait of this site, so:

Profiles that say "I'm not being rude or ignorant if I don't reply, I just don't think you're my type" - well I couldn't disagree more!
It IS rude, so don't be surprised if you get a sarcastic follow up message if you blank my first polite one after viewing me.

If you have trust issues because of your ex and assume that I'm going to be the same before you have even met me, then please don't contact me, why would you even be on a dating site in the first place if you're not sure that you're ready to date again?

I would want to speak to someone on the phone

before meeting them in the flesh because due to my own fault, I didn't follow my own rule and have ended up on a date where its hard work trying to get a conversion out of a person when I've met them. Please put your phone down sometimes when on a date, it's not nice trying to talk to the side of someone's head.

If you feel that there's no spark, I'd rather you told me straight, I'm big enough and ugly enough to handle it, better than me having to go to the loo to give you the chance to think of some 'sudden family emergency' that you have to attend so that you can leave. To be honest though that does me a favour because it shows that you have a deceitful streak, which means I dodged a bullet really.

Meet Me, why click on me then not respond to my polite message thanking you? or worse still, block me when I do? Are you not wired up right?

Text speak: When I get messages like "Hi, how R U', I just look at them and think 'Well what the heck am I supposed to do with that?'

Really sorry about having to put that as it makes me look like a right moaner lol but I gave in and felt like it had to be said.

I'd really rather not do email relationships - if you aren't prepared to talk on the phone if and when should you feel comfortable to do so, then I'm not really interested. Typing on a phone is a pain!

I'm here to make friends or more, which means that there has to be some form of physical contact at some point and a phone call is the next stage a while after initial contact on here

I don't need to say what I'm looking for because I don't have a type, it doesn't matter if you're blonde, brunette, slim, not so slim, short or tall if the spark is there :-) I know that I'm hardly George Clooney, so I'm not arrogant enough to have high demands.

I'm not guilty of this thankfully, but you ladies who say you don't want to see pics of guys with cars, fish, gym pics etc, why do you think we'd be interested in seeing your pets or horse? Or even worse, those stupid snapchat filters where you have flowers around your head or dog ears and tongue?

Thank you for reading and it would be lovely to hear from you x"

Having finally reached the end of the gentlemen's profile, I was word-blind, and more than a little fearful of how a message from me might be received. So, I played safe and went for a coffee and a biscuit, instead of messaging him.

The need to conform to too many demands was becoming another no-go area.

MIKE

"I went out with a cornflake once. She accused me of being a cereal dater .....

****** UPDATE ******
Just bought a bike. Need a cycle buddy :-)
Oi !!! I said Cycle :-o

****** RANT Section ******

Welcome to :
youbetterhaveplentyofmoneyandagreatjoborforgetit.com (Jesus, shallowest place on earth). A large percentage on here need to be on Sugardaddy.com.

No, i don't have issues and don't need you to tell me. If you take offence, I've obviously hit a nerve and you are the one who should take a look at yourself.

Oh, and lighten up ladies. So many lacking a sense of humour .....

End of rants, for now ;-) ...... Please read on xx

Normal good bloke, seeking the same (with lady bits I hope ;-)).
I hate the phrase "Lads". I hate the concept of lads. Hence, I'm NOT a Lad.
Grew up overseas (South Africa). Would ideally love a relationship, but would also be nice to make some new friends.
I've old fashioned views, good morals. Not a career guy or big earner, pay my way. I know that means 99% gone. Oh well, you could be that 1%er xx

Job : Pharmaceuticals Production - work shifts (pay my own bills)
Build : average
Height : 6' (honest, I really am. Bring your tape measure - height only)
Eyes : blue
Hair : dark (greying)
Facial hair : sorry, no beard, just stubble
Tattoos : sorry, none (I don't follow, I'm not a sheep)
Accent : neutral - not Bolton. Some think I sound posh. I can assure you, I'm not. Wish I was though ??

Intelligent : yes

General knowledge : excellent

Sense of humour : quick, sarcastic

Car/home : yes

Kids : none, but not against, just never happened and I couldn't eat a whole one ;-)

Married : never

Pets : none, dog lover though

Smoke : never (don't lie, it's very obvious who does)

Drink : rarely, but not against a bit more

Interests : most usual things. Have a bit of a passion for Africa's fauna & flora. It's in my heart, always will be.

Ps. Bought all the camping gear, but yet to try it out.

Pps. I know how to Braai (bbq), it's from my upbringing.

If I don't reply, no offence meant. I just don't think we're compatible (most likely distance). It happens to us all. good luck xx"

Two things stood out for me with this fine specimen: firstly, I smoke, so he wouldn't like me. But, more noteworthy than that was the rant. I've found plenty that rant, and perhaps with good reason, depending on their experiences. For me, however, it sends a red flag: no matter what you might think, sometimes it's probably better to keep it to yourself, at least until you know the person a little. Otherwise, it just makes you look like you don't have the ability to let things go - in a relationship, that is pretty important.

SID

"Hopeless romantic looking for genuine, trustworthy and loving lady."

A short one, but the photo was lovely, so I messaged and eagerly awaited the reply. My excitement sizzled as I saw that he had responded, then fizzled as I read him asking for the size of my boobs! It was a good way to find out how the blocking tool worked.

CONNOR

"This is the tough bit. I haven't had to update my CV for twenty years, so I am rusty at this sort of thing!

I'm pretty sporty. I used to be obsessed with football, playing rather than watching, but it's a cruel sport for 40+ year olds! So I try other pursuits which are less vulnerable to dodgy hamstrings such as cricket, golf and cycling. I'm not obsessed by any of these, but they are good fun and fill a gap!

I enjoy going out, don't we all, (apologies agoraphobics), and I love a meal out or a decent pub! I like to travel, but have not done that enough. I'd love to find that someone special to explore new places with!

I'm a funny guy, I'll make you laugh! I promise! If I don't I'll pay for your cab home!

Ok, how did I do? This is a revamped profile. It's better than before, but no doubt not as good as it could be. Message me and let's chat! X"

Ignoring the love of golf, it appeared that I had found someone who liked to travel. Could this be the man for me? So, off my message went.

A response!

I responded back, and so did he; was I onto something? Might this lead to a date? With my heart fluttering, I waited for further mail… and waited… and waited… and… well, waited...

So many do this, which is so frustrating and, in my mind, plain rude. When you seem to have been communicating well, this sends a message in itself: that they are shallow, and obviously not worthy of your time.

I pulled my big-girl pants up higher, and carried on the search.

GUY

"A man with depth! What is this? I can't comprehend! I'm confused! Well let me explain....

I do life differently, always the non-conformist. Always looking for that 'different girl' the one here for the right reasons (not sure she is to be found on here)

Im the one your mum would love and your dad would trust. Highly positive, Immensely passionate and expressive. Funny, cheeky and eccentric.

Im the lover and the clown, The one that picks you up when you fall down. (unintentional rhyme, but so bloody pleased with myself)

My life in 30 seconds, 10 seconds if you read fast and 0 seconds if you cant be bothered because its 3am and you cant sleep :)

Brought up in Australia.... Cool. With the odd hot day.

Fantastic childhood.... Broken bones, grazed knees and a life outside.

Got educated.... What a dangerous mistake that was.

Freelance Graphic Designer/Digital Artist Blogger and trying that Writer thing.... So friggin blessed.

Two teenage boys and a Border Collie.... Not so friggin blessed.

I take Mondays off so I don't get that Monday morning feeling.... Inspired.

Now I get that Tuesday morning feeling.... And I never thought that one through.

Can disappear at 2am.... dirty little fridge raider.

Only to find blachberry yoghurts left.... Heart broken and very disappointed.

Went fishing once and caught a whopper...
sorry no picture.

Bared my chest and stuck out my tongue
once.,.. sorry still no picture of that.

Stood by my shiny car too.... you guessed it,
still no picture of that.

I'm guessing I best end this before it turns into an Operators/Health and Safety manual. I have hopes, I have dreams and future plans. I dont think a few words or pictures will ever tell the whole story. It's all about taking that chance and chance could be just around the corner if we open your eyes. Xx"

A spark of humour, and what appeared to be an honest start to the proceedings!

All started well: we swapped messages for a while, but then he stopped. Well used to this by now, I continued onward, without his sparkling repartee.

Then, lo and behold, he started messaging again. I responded, a few more days of conversation passed, then… yes, he stopped again.

By this point, I had started to talk to someone, so had left the site, to see how that developed. After two more profiles, I trekked back into the pool. And… up he pops again!

To my knowledge, he has now been looking for at least eight years. Maybe he needs to learn how to finish a conversation!

MICHAEL

"The greatest thing you'll ever learn, Is just to love and be loved in return"

Are you looking for - A Generous, Career Driven, Independent ,Quick witted, well balanced, Caring, Healthy ,Family Oriented Man, who can hold a good conversation, and still has his own teeth and hair ?
You have come to the right place !

So about me - I have never been married (came close) I have never had kids,and I am not on the run from Interpol !
I have though, been blessed with 4 wonderful sisters (so I am used to being bossed about - lol)

Love my job, working as a Currency Bank Trader in The Financial Markets.
Sorry, but I am all out of macho photos of me climbing Mount Everest, fighting a wild Tiger or parking my Lamborghini.
I keep fairly fit, but I am not obsessed
You wont find me staring at myself, admiring

my body in the mirror dreaming of a six pack !

High maintenance, Moody, False women, need not apply. Just an Amazing Woman - You know who you are !

Michael
X

There are quite a few of this type of profile: lightweight on what he would like. Does he believe that women might actually think of themselves as “high maintenance”, “moody” or “false”, because I’m sure that none of us do? It’s a bit like writing: “All men who fart too much, hog too much of the duvet, and are boring, aren’t welcome.” Which man is going to sit there and say: “Oh, yes, I’m boring; I’d better not message her!”?

JOHN

> *"Hi I'm John, I never know what to put in these things. I'm half English half Italian. I'm looking to meet a down to earth girl and just see where things go. Oh and I'm wearing sunglasses a lot cause I have photophobia, which basically means my eyes are really sensitive to light."*

Okay, fair enough, John; I understand why you are hiding your lovely eyes. But, what I didn't see coming was his age: having established that there was a twenty-five-year age gap (in his favour) I swiftly moved on! Why? Because my daughter would have a fit, and explaining it to my friends would involve many nods and tales of being taken advantage of - that's *me* being taken advantage of, not him! Age is always going to be a factor.

My search was set for 42 to 62-year-olds. Many (though very cute, it has to be said) would have a profile age of 50-something, but one look at the picture would lead me to doubt that, and consider whether I wanted to be out with someone who was constantly being looked at. Not to mention whether or not he looked smart enough in his school uniform!

Age is relevant to life experience; I wanted to be with someone who had gained enough to have views, knowledge and hold a reasoned debate, without having to check online for his facts.

JERRY

"I like everything and anything"

Hmmm.

Given a lack of interests, in a profile like this, how does one start a conversation? Surely, it helps to be just a tiny bit more specific in your quest.

I actually messaged one man, who had very a similar bio to this, and asked outright what his specific interests were: the answer, apparently, was "Everything!" Nowhere really to go from that.

JUSTIN

"Firstly: You're instincts are correct - I am younger than it says...

Anyway... I sleep once a day and always dream about sharks. I won the sack race every year in primary school. I have made extraordinary five course banquets using only a spatula and a toaster. I'm a black belt in spooning and give out world class cuddles. Brad Pitt stole my red jacket for the filming of Fight Club. Curry is my favourite food group. I can bake a cake in 5 minutes dead. Animals love me but Fish hate me. On the third Wednesday of every month I repair unicycles free of charge. I never perspire except on Sundays. My strengths outweigh my weaknesses.

Likes:
Dancing, dance music, 80's music, 80's films, absinthe, rum, bloody marys, penguins, football, writing, lizards, chillis, turkish delight, travel, white russians, dinosaurs"

I found that my head was starting to spin by this point, and that I might require more than a cup of tea to get to the end…

"Dislikes:

Sprouts, cider, sloths, bad dancers, flies, R n B, honey badgers, flip flops, people who call ladybirds 'ladybugs'

Do NOT message me if:

1, You think super Mario is cooler than Sonic.

2, Your favourite Bond is Pierce Brosnan.

About Me

For all you 'pouters' out there, here's a silly thing wot I wrote about

Online girl

Online girl, I like your style,
That pout of yours made me stare for a while,
Your technicolor blouse gave me cause to think,
Do I prefer green, or do I prefer pink?

The way it gapes open in front of you,
I reckon you've lost a button or two,
But that shape looks all wrong, makes me feel,
Either I need glasses or those boobs aren't real

Online girl, I have to admire,

Your eco-warrior profile, it sets me on fire,
Your evident concern for your fellow man,
Your refreshing willingness to embrace fake tan

That picture of yours is a cracker for sure,
It makes you look sexy and hot, not demure,
But I've been here a while, so pin back your ears,
You've been using that photo for at least seven years!

Online girl, you made me light in the head,
With that shot, half naked, sprawled on your bed,
I'm not super tidy, I have to confess,
*But frankly your bedroom's a right f***king mess!*

You say in your profile, "take me seriously please!"
Your tired of those pervs who just want to squeeze,
But have you considered, it might serve you best,
To show less of your booty and cover that chest

Your skin looks so smooth, your daily regime
Must include all kinds, of lotions and cream
But wait, there's no pores on your face, at the top
Stop using that Snapchat, use less photoshop

I see you're 'low maintenance', wants a man who is 'real'
You're just as content, in wellie or heel
Happy on the sofa with wine and DVD
You get 2 out of 10 for original-i-tee

But I'm judging again, I need to come clean
I need to confess, I'm not all that I seem
My age is a lie, my height, some way off
My teeth are all bent and my toupee falls off

But let's pass on our failings, embrace what's 'unique',
Life's really too short, we're both past our peak,
See past my squint teeth, my shiny bald head,
I'll not mention your weight...until we're in bed

We seem so well matched in so many ways,
You're needs are so few, just wine and sun

rays,
*Your loathing for d***pics, players and twats,*
Your fondness for period dramas....and cats

Online girl, we've been texting all day,
I'm ready to meet you, to talk drink and play,
The teasing is over, let's meet up tonight,
I'll boast "I'm well hung", you'll say "don't talk shite!"

Affable, falable, secure, creative, contradictory, independent, curious, philosophical, naughty, playful, cynical, cheeky, optimistic, talented, useless but fearless

I live a fairly quiet life, punctuated by momentary lapses of hedonistic, joyful indulgence, regular travel and occasional Angel Delight.

I avoid fertility (fully functioning ovaries) but am paradoxically fearful of scalpels. I'm looking for (in order of importance, intelligence, character and beauty.

I appreciate unambiguous waistlines,

conversation, consideration and cake. Delights in dogs. Loves poignant profanity. Prefer strong women (mentally!)

Dislikes excessive denim, monobrows and similarly hirsute tendencies, inauthentic or affected types, unkind, inconsiderate, superficial or delusional people (supercool? No thanks)

Likes: people with integrity and humility,

52 not 50, Pisces not Aquarius
And.....No piccy - no talky! (all my pictures are recent)

I've been dating on and off for a few years now, so I've been through the universal phases of excitement and apathy, flurries of groundhog-day-like activity and long periods of complete inactivity. I've dated all over the UK and abroad, met some lovely people and had both frivolous and loving relationships lasting from a few weeks to 4 years (not counting a 15yr marriage) I've also made a few great and mutually supportive friendships with people

> *who I initially dated so even at this stage I'm still optimistic that online dating can be a good thing.*
>
> *That said, I now tend to date less frequently and closer to home, (Winchester). Love is very elusive but I'm hopeful the best is still to come. I am by nature, an optimist."*

No, I never got to the end; I stopped reading after learning of Justin's dislikes of honey badgers and sloths. I mean, really!

SIMON

> *"Hi thanks for dropping by. I'm a 47 year old male who is very single. Not had much luck dating maybe that can change on here ."*

Although I wasn't sure of the difference between being single and being "very single", I must have been having a bad day, so I sent off a nice, light and breezy message.

His response came back, asking about body and boob size. And, he wonders why he has no luck?

GRANT

> *"Hi everyone recently updated as i was being blocked by people id never contacted so presume my profile was gazumped lol im easy going normal guy ' friendly ' intelligent and love all forms of coversation. I have many interests if you want to know more feel free to ask thank you for looking a girlfriend once said "" you never take me anywhere expensive" i said get your coat" she said where we going """ i said the petrol station ha ha ;;;i said to my wife why dont you ever tell me when you come "" she said i dont like phoning you when im at work ;,;: theres a gangster by me who keeps pulling peoples pants up his names weggie kray lol"*

I like a sense of humour in a man, but having read this gent's, it didn't take much to understand why people were blocking him: humour is one thing, but for me he just took it too far.

I moved on.

DEAN

"April

Looking for a 'brexit buddy.....(stress relief... (from being collectively f$#&Ed))

Update 9 March:

Old injury (nudist beach, Greece 15 years ago....I still can't walk straight!)forces me to do less at gym & it never works out meeting people in bars...too much alcohol means making bad decisions....hmmmmm...I"ve 'grown')....(possibly 'awoken' (hopefully 'enlightened'))...so I'll try his again.....it can't have got worse can it? ??

Still doing 4 exercise classes on Fridays (body combat, pilates, senior keep fit (I'm the 'baby' in the class...(mostly)) & aquafit) & Wendy's Wednesdays Weirdos (/wonders) ..(yoga, body boost & aquafit.)

I'm back into bars & bands with the time this has freed up (the lounge in boldmere tonight if you're free!...(It's a Beatles/ Rolling Stones cover bands night)..

I'm looking for someone pleasant and presentable..(or at least tries occasionally)

An interest in errrrr.....bananas, chilli's,wwf & HIT would be advantageous..(??)..though not essential. (training available for the right candidate....??)

(Probably books to...the internet is so 'passe')

Anyway this should be enough to pique your interest (or not)...the rest is nonsense from before...so don't bother reading it (unless you're bored....but as i'"ve forgotten most of it (or wrote it while drunk) I bear no responsibility for it's contents...any similarities to real events or people are purely coincidental)

(Hopefully that should do it....??)

Woohoo! Single again (26th Aug '18)! Got to lay low at the gym for a while in case I run into 'Verucca' again..(because I picked her up in the sauna ...??) (She said I looked 'hot'.....in a sauna..I fall for the cheesiest lines huh?). So not looking for chat...just dates...more updates later. (& Oi! Judy.,.. there's no point adding me as a favourite when your settings won't allow me to message you..??)

Woohoo! Met someone in the sauna (at the gym ...I'm calling her verruca as I(happily) can't get rid of her)... Hopefully you'll all be invited to the wedding...but as it's only been 5 days (& she's not on here) I can dream away...?? So goodbye , good luck & happy 'fishing'...??

yeay new year..new start (etc) perhaps a yearly round up would be easier as monthly seems to much time to invest in online relationships going nowhere (see below)...so (to be short(-est) and sweet(-est))...

.swm (solvent)..(no, not the water sort), no (applicable) (emotional) baggage would like date (hopefully) leading to more....

Yeay christmas...lots of free time to fill..whaddya wanna do?
(The rest is rubbish...dont read it...too difficult to delete ...phone app)

Yeay Halloween!
I suppose I should try monthly updates (again! POF is getting 'pushy')
So...

October (30th)

Busy summer! (Thanks for asking) (IT'll mke sense (?) 'if ' you read to the bottom..

The headline's from 'The Cleveland Show' and I'm not (really) 'a millionaire space unicorn' (that's from 'Family Guy' and errrr..a bit of Russel Brand) but I do like to keep 'busy'.

Anyway I never got around to posting my 'troll' piece from my 'adventures' (on here)

back in May so I'l lrectify that now (if I can find it) and the rest of it's from errrr...before(?) if this hasn't 'whetted' your appetite (piqued your interest?)I wouldn't bother with the rest of the stdff I'm too lazy(/busy?) to delete. Or reread it. Or edit it in general.It's better to just leave it out there in all it's 'glory' (updating does shove stuff out the other end though....just imagine the 'insights you've missed)

(note to self check 'armpit licking' has gone) (and not to 'press' update until I've edited this in the WP window)

And remember to come back next month y'all!

Can't find the 'Troll Report'

but found this (after reading about an english

girl winning a haiku competiton) (in the guardian if you're that google happy)
August...

'Daily Haikus, (for some of you's),to peruse...
And a return to overpunctuating!
(' national level of annoyance rises')

'Tis a gift from god,
that a prince from a frog can
be found in this b(l)og!'

'Probably best to
skıp the rest, (unless you are,
An insect (or pest)

Firstly...
Read the rules/conversation starter..(too many complaints that I'm wasting people's time (?))
Secondly...I recommend you don't read this. You'll regret it. (And if you do, don't blame me. You were warned.)
And
Thirdly....Don't contact me!
(unless it's nice)
(I'm sure you have a sense of humour

somewhere in there)
FM! 10 days in and it's not getting any better (pmsl.x.)
June 11th...Boo! Batman's dead...(there goes another bit of my childhood...)
Election update...'twas an oxymoron election...Corbyn lost (but won more seats) and the 'other' one won (but lost some seats).
(Also Corbyn was accused of being 'in bed ' with terrorists and then May (the 'other' one) joins forces with them...(you won't be reading that in the papers soon) (or will you?)..(it depends on what you read I suppose..)

Anyway another (Saturday night 'in' (playing with my 'Baba Ganoush' (photos on request... (it's a lovely 'shade' of purple too..(and so shiny!). My 'secret' is ......(it's 'full' skin (in)) + ('something'else')..
(And if you think that's 'risque' you should 'see' what I can do with a 'banana')..

June 8th ....looking good...

EMERGENCY (June (7th)) UPDATE!

FOURTHLY, YES! VOTE CORBYN!

Or the dog (Henri) gets it...he's 10 (& 1/2) and has ruined my love life...(he smells, shits loads and the slobber has ruined the 'decor' of my house (and when 'guests ' come back my 'allure' is left 'wanting' (sob!))

(can't be much of a surprise)

(I don't expect that to increase my response (or quality of response) rate....but you have to take a stand somewhere....(well actually, I also joined the 'Labour Party' to get JC elected but you 'get ' what I mean...))

(He can't actually read!)

(So he doesn't really 'need' glasses!)

(His life span is actually 8yrs..(if they can get past congenital abnormalities that kill them at approx 3 yrs...)

(and he snores...)

'Anyway as be
fore...the rest (the past/thoughts)
is for you to explore'.........

Anyway it's too soul destroying to bother with this crap (how do you put up with it?)

If you're serious about dating contact me

through FB (I'm on the committee of Rookery Park Friends (Erdington...sign up to our group..and state that you don't want the manor house turned into 'private' housing (William Wilberforce's wife lived there ffs (slavery abolitionist?..also there's lots of 'redwoods' that apparently Thomas Jefferson planted).
(I don't mind being trolled there because our 'chair' works for the council and wants it sold off anyway (and she controls the FB account...p

Conversation Starters (i.e. what you'd like to do on a first date...)
Didn't this used to be first date ideas (or something similar)... Anyway ..vintage clothes shopping.,fooling around in the library & lunch/gambling in the pub /bookies followed by (if all goes well) a night dancing ('a vertical expression of a horizontal desire'(O.W.)) in aforementioned vintage clothes...
(Style & affordability over 'fashion any day)

Anyway the rest of this is (probably) nonsense too....so errrrr...you've finished....decision time...??

coffee shop (or pub)
(possibly (hour) long walk)
No more (unpleasant) timewasters (/nutters) ....
(please?)

(hmmmm....tough crowd)
Right I'm hijacking this bit for 'rules'
so errrr...
RULES!
(I'm upsetting the 'trolls'(apparently) so I thought it might help (them)... but errrr...a lot of them seem to think they're errrr... 'normal' (and it'll stop me repeating in the main bit ...1o years (on here) to learn that... but hey ho ...I got there in the end) (and more space for my 'marvelous' musings'..hurray!
I might go full on BJ (Bridget Jones ffs...) and stt adding weight, booze, etc...12st 3lbs (thanks for asking/thinking) (5'10"(and a half))
Also my 'headlines' tend to be rubbish so if anyone wans to suggest a better one (after reading this) then I'll publish it (Alice in Wonderland on Acid was a comment I received, that's definitley the best comment so far...hmmmmm) (I have a winner for week ending 19th)(then)..

TROLL RULES!

1. Be nice (and if you can't be nice be careful)

2.Be polite. (you're only winding yourself up...I'll just find it funny)

3. Enjoy yourself. (you only live once (unless you're a Buddhist) (another type of Budddhist than me) (this 'column' is an attempt to achieve Buddhahood (thereby breaking the cycle of rebirth)

(yes, it is...)

4. Be fair

I've just worked out how to stop repeating myself on 'About You'. (Well rereading the whole thing would help. As would editing but where's the fun in that?)

I don't mind 'trolls' but tend not to 'feed' them or they keep coming back.

You need to understand that POF's an oxymoron. It's a dating site where no one ever dates. (well..rarely). I imagined it to be like on 'Friends' the TV show where it's considered good manners to date at least 3 times. (People seem to want to find 'the one' right there and then). (And it's costing me a fortune!)

If you want an 'internet' date then I'm always

available to play a few games (exclusively) for an hour (or so). Scrabble and WWF have chat and I feel that the only way to save my sanity on POF is to not come on every day this time around (possibly weekly). I love backgammon too (and chess) but it's timed. (So difficult to chat)

'You can discover more about a person in an hour of play than in a year of conversation' (Plato (supposedly)).

What else? Oh yes the recent stuff is written while listening to Bruno Mars (Just The way You Are, and 'Marry You' (it's about commitment and impulsiveness:

And, there was young Dean!

Can you understand what he's on about, throughout most of his profile? Answers on a postcard, please.

*

My extensive reading of profiles did, at least, give me something to do on my quiet evenings, even if nothing would come of it.

And, yes, I do hold my hands up to "borrowing" from some of them, to enhance my own details, until a few months down the line, my profile read something along the lines of:

> *"Rather than talk about myself, I thought I would ask people around me for their views.*
> *This is what they said:*
> *Best friend: 'Not you again!'*
> *Daughter: 'You're my mother; I have to like you.'*
> *Bank Manager: 'Please call into the branch to discuss your current situation.'*
> *Checkout girl at my local shop: 'Please stop asking me stupid questions; I have a job to do!'*
> *If you'd like to find out the truth for yourself, send me a message."*

…but, did it work?

6. First dates

Well, it had to happen eventually, I guess.

Having messaged one gentleman for several weeks, and built up some confidence in the process of online dating, it was time to take it into the real world.

After arranging to meet in an open place, with lots of people around, we arrived at the same time - an excellent start. Much better than the next three hours, in which he talked non-stop about himself, without any interest in finding out about me. Finally, pleading a work commitment, I permitted a kiss on the cheek and ran for home.

My arrival back home was greeted with a message from *Mr. I Can't Stop Talking*, saying how much he had enjoyed the date. I pondered my response and, although I hate lying, felt that a little white one was in order: I explained that I didn't feel I was ready for the dating scene, at this point in my life.

The second date was with a lovely man, who had made me laugh through his messages and appeared to be the "real McCoy". It was such a shame that the chemistry just wasn't there for us and, with no ill feelings, on he swam.

My third and final date had taken months of hilarious, informative messaging, to try to arrange a meeting for us between work commitments; he was working nights and I had a heavy teaching load. But, the day finally arrived and, with nerves jumping and hands shaking, I found myself waiting outside a pub for him to arrive.

Mr. Tall, Dark and Handsome was *absolutely* as I had imagined and hoped he would be, and over the next two hours I fell in love!

Within weeks, we were making plans to move in together, and the daughter was happily planning her new social life, without Mother in tow. Our first Christmas as a family was brilliant, and our plans intensified, through our common interest to travel. With huge smiles and love in our hearts, we set off to travel the world…

So, really my story should end here.

But, life isn't like that.

After four and a half amazing years of travel, and life-changing decisions - which included moving to another country - *Mr. Tall, Dark and Handsome* was diagnosed with cancer. My life shattered to pieces.

In our final moments together, we looked back at our pictures and recounted the happiest of the times we had shared… all thanks to online dating.

*

It took a long time - several years, in fact - to even consider entering the dating scene once more.

But, knowing that the online world had worked before, and believing, in my heart, I dug through the drawers to find my big-girl pants, and once more ventured in.

7. Second time around

Older and wiser, with a few battle scars, I set about constructing a new profile. Having loaded it with a small selection of current pictures, my rod was baited and the fishing could commence.

This time, though, there was one even larger hurdle (yes, even bigger than my fussy list of what was acceptable): the fact that I was now living abroad; the only way to meet someone in the flesh would be for one or the other of us to get on a plane - that should test the mettle of someone who really liked me!

I found that life hadn't changed much in the online dating world, seeing *Mr. I've Been On Here For Years*'s picture, as soon as I logged on. I moved swiftly onward, and took up the hobby of reading profiles all over again. Within the hour, it was if no time had passed at all. Most of the same men were still there!

My first message, which I received within minutes, caught me off-guard:

"You look cute. I have twelve inches I could give you."

After my brain engaged in any logical way, my response was sent:

"Thanks, but I already have a ruler."

Patting myself on the back, I launched my line back into the water and hoped that my fish would swim by.

A few months passed, along with a lot of messaging - some which had led to conversations; others which were swiftly ignored.

I found myself talking to a lovely man, from my original hometown.

He knew that I was not in the country but, rather than being put off, he seemed happy to embrace the opportunity, and booked a flight to come and see me.

Mr. Lovely arrived and the week sped past; we got on like a house on fire, laughing and giggling away, like schoolchildren. We started to talk about how we could manage a future together, and he left knowing that this might go the distance, given my travelling background (which, since first going online, had changed dramatically, from initially travelling only during school holidays, to now travelling all the time).

His only tie was his dog, but we had discussed this, and were both happy to wait, until he could join me full-time on the road. It was sad when he lost his ageing pet, and although my heart broke for him, I was secretly delighted that it could mean a much earlier arrival of the start of our full life together.

It is strange to me, why people do some things.

I did understand, to a degree, but couldn't help but feel upset when he announced that he was getting a puppy. I wasn't sure where the puppy would fit in.

Having pointed that out, in a most delicate manner, he then informed me that the travel was too much for him, anyway!

When I last heard about him, he was still looking for love, but now has a kitten to help. Not sure where the puppy idea went, but surely a kitten would be even more difficult to get into a rucksack!

8. The French connection

Having partly given up on dating, and spent a lot of time carrying my backpack around Europe, I found myself working as a volunteer in France.

So, with evenings to fill, I considered the French connection, taking up the slightly arduous job of translating profiles, from French into English.

Who knew that French men were so into bricolage (D.I.Y. in my world), and that so many were widows? Many, though, did take exceedingly good photos, and I found myself faced with some very handsome profiles to read – yes, it appeared that I was back to being shallow again!

Several conversations were struck but, for one reason or another, it just wasn't the right fit for me. Although ignoring the impassioned responses to my rejection was pretty tough, I hardened my heart and started chatting to a man who appeared to want the same things in life as me.

Mr. France corresponded well in English, and I felt a rapport was building up. We had discussed travel, and had been in agreement about travelling the world. But somehow, the *children question* hadn't been asked, until it fell into one of his conversations - you might remember my thoughts on bringing young children into my life. Now, a good few years further down the line, and with my lovely daughter enjoying her independence, I couldn't see that a young family would work, with my backpacking way of life.

I asked the question (well, I had to): "How old is your daughter?" I kept my fingers crossed that she was grown up and didn't need adult supervision.

The answer arrived: "One is five and the other is ten. They are wonderful children and would love to have you as their mother."

WHAT!!? How had this important information been missed, for so many weeks?

So, *Miss Selfish* (me) took her time in replying, trying to be as gentle as she could. The message went very much along the lines of:

"Sorry, not going to happen! Good luck."

I didn't expect to hear back.

Then, a few days passed, before a message appeared. Mr. France said that he was sorry for taking a while to reply, but his daughter had been rushed into hospital.

I'm not an uncaring or nasty person (contrary to how it may seem), and my empathetic self drafted a message, sending my sympathies and asking what had happened. As my mind pictured car accidents, falls and broken bones, Mr. France went on to explain that his daughter had refused to eat, because I had rejected her and wouldn't be her mother!

Oh, heck! Oh, my! What was I to say to that? Should I reply at all? The dilemma nagged at the back of my mind.

Then, the teacher in me spoke out, and I sent my final communication, saying that I was sorry – and that maybe in his future dating life he shouldn't mention such things to his children, until he had actually met the women concerned, and discussed it with her first… I didn't hear back.

9. The on-and-off type and getting started

One thing that I have never understood - and still don't - is those times when I have been messaging someone for a couple of days, all seems to be going well, then suddenly all communication stops dead. Have I said something to offend them? Have they had an accident? More likely, a prettier face has come along, and they have just moved on a little faster than I have. It is particularly frustrating, when you think it was going well.

One friend - who was also fishing in the watery depths - expressed this in a rather nice way: "Sweets. It's a sweet shop; as soon as a new flavour arrives, that becomes the favourite." Which, of course, rules me out immediately, being a bit of a humbug. It also poses the question of why people are so shallow in their intentions.

Starting conversations can be problematic. I have found that the best way forward is to find something in common and ask questions about that. But, if their profile is sadly lacking in content, then you may be reduced to asking how they are finding the site, leaving yourself exposed to several messages bemoaning how many bitches there are online, and realizing that they are not actually interested in you - only their own experience. Because travel was now my main occupation, I tended to only message men who had that listed in their hobbies, or their written text.

My starting point would lean towards: *"Where have you travelled to?"* A nice, easy route into a long conversation, I would have thought. How wrong can you be?

Responses have included:

"Everywhere", which just astounds me – for someone to have visited all 193 countries already! Go them!

"I've stopped travelling and don't want to do anymore." Fair enough, although baffling to me, as I can't imagine stopping.

"Up your skirt!" Well, as my backpack doesn't contain a skirt, and you're obviously after something that I'm not giving, that's not going to go far.

A couple of times, my opening gambit has been answered well, and conversation has flowed - until they stop dead and I hear nothing more. Maybe they're off travelling and decided to leave me behind?

Weeks and weeks can pass by, of on and off conversations and interactions - some of only a few messages - before my realization that the person wasn't going to turn out to be Mr. Right, or that I have been given false hope. A few led me to believe that they would be happy to chat, but only, it turned out, when they were bored; I would only hear from them every now and then. Wouldn't it be so much easier if we were all more honest about things? I wondered this, constantly.

I must be getting caustic in my older years. One gent, who had messaged twice in one day, then left six weeks to pass, before asking for my number in his third message. I gave my usual response to this request: *"Sorry, I would want to know more about you before giving out my personal details."* A reasonable response, in my mind. For his further benefit, I added: *"Given your response time, this might take several years!"*

On my first foray into the online world, I did, however, start talking to a great guy, with whom to this day I still keep in touch as friends, even though we have never met. He left the pond and met the love of his life, whilst filling his car with petrol. Maybe I should check out the petrol stations, spending an evening at my local B.P.!

My pet hate became those who use text-speak. I know I'm shallow and may be a snob now, but the ability to form a sentence with some structure and grammar is important to me. I have even added this to my list of requirements in a man... the list which is growing ever longer.

10. No sex, please – we're British!

I have no issue with sex, nor those who are seeking only that. However, it is helpful for them to say this at the outset.

Most of the online apps now have an option to put in your intentions - I always go for those *"looking for a relationship"*, and will ignore profiles which state only *"looking for fun"*. That given, why do men still message, then, asking for a one-night stand? I much prefer the man who comes out with it at the start, so I don't waste my time conversing any further.

One gentleman – *Mr. Bar Owner* - had messaged me for a while and things seem to be progressing. He liked travel (tick); he didn't have young children (tick); he had hair (tick); and, he was tall (big tick). A few weeks had passed, and we had discussed a huge variety of topics, so I started to consider moving things along a little, and suggested meeting up.

"Great," said Mr. Bar Owner, *"we can have sex in the cellar of my gaffe."*

How do I get it so wrong? I constantly ask myself.

Consider the poor customers, drinking his beer!

Profiles which mention handcuffs and domination are ones

which I avoid, but still this doesn't deter the gentleman from messaging me, and then continuing to add me as a "favourite", even though I have responded with my usual: *"Sorry, not for me. Good luck."* The block button really is a great tool.

But, I have yet to find a dating site which allows me to block a user without:

a) having sent a message;

or

b) having liked them first.

This seems a slight oversight, in my view - my case in point being men who favourite you, yet don't read your profile. You remove them as a favourite, and they favourite you again; you remove them again and they favourite you yet again… and, so on and so forth. Stalking tendencies spring to mind when a man does this. The only way to stop them is to like them and then block them, which, of course, gives them false hope, as you pray that your wi-fi remains stable for long enough that you can block them, before they start messaging you back!

11. Third time lucky!

"Very cute. Can be riled when removed from chocolate source, lacks any sense of direction, terrible at packing and always overweight at check in. Reads for hours, letting you watch the football in peace. Wonderful for spooning; talks..... a lot."

My latest contribution to profiles. How would this fare in the ocean of fish?

12. Swipe this way

Having left my dating life in abeyance and picked up my rucksack, I returned to the U.K. six months later, to start a summer position. I thought that a date or two might provide me with something to look forward to, after the long shifts.

My hook was baited, but things had moved on in the online dating world. With new sites aplenty, I adjusted my profile, pulled up my big-girl pants and joined the masses in the world of swiping pictures.

So many left swipes went past, with an occasional break to read a profile, because I could now see who had "liked" me. I thought that by liking them back I might be onto a winner… Wrong. You might match, but it appeared that men expected you to make the first move in the messaging. Being slightly old-fashioned in my views of dating, I took the bull by the horns and asked a couple of matches: *"Why match but not message?"* There was no response from one, whilst the other messaged back, saying that he didn't know he had to!

Profiles became my reading material once more. These sites allow an opportunity to state your relationship status and sexuality; all information is good information. Until I realized that many were in *"complicated"* relationships, and *"sexually open"*. With no wish to compromise someone else's relationship, I passed them by, and kept on swiping…

JIM'S PERSONAL INFO

I'm SO glad the world did not end. I still have so many unanswered questions! I never found out who let the dogs out, the way to get to Sesame Street, why Dora doesn't just use Google maps, why we don't ever see the headline "Psychic Wins Lottery", why women can't put on mascara with their mouth closed, why "abbreviated" is such a long word, why lemon juice is made with artificial flavor yet dishwashing liquid is made with real lemons, why they sterilize the needle for lethal injections and why do you have to "put your two cents in" but it's only a "penny for your thoughts"? Where's that extra penny going to? Why did Joanie love Chachi? If a deaf person has to go to court is it still called a hearing? Does the alphabet song and twinkle twinkle little star have the same tune? Why did you just try to sing those two previous songs? And just what is Victoria's secret? You see, the world just has to keep going. I have too many questions...... and do you really think I am this witty ????

Relationship: I'm single

Sexuality: I'm straight

Appearance: Average body

Living: By myself

Children: Grown up

Drinking: I drink socially

Always a draw when a person makes you laugh. Still chuckling away, I matched and messaged.

It seems that things really haven't changed: no response was forthcoming.

PETER'S PERSONAL INFO

OK so here we go, Im a very decent guy with no baggage and am who you see in the picture, confident, solvent great sense of humour and available now, Im not looking for quantity just quality and a casual relationship and dating with a woman who is confident and comfortable in her skin. Im not a serial dater as said just looking for quality and definitely not quantity, I m experience in life and know what Im looking for.

OK please read and don't be offended by my requirements, Im not out to waste my time so if you don't fit the requirements just move on.

Please don't send me a message with "Hey There " as IM not interested in small talk or making friends I have enough friends.
If you the type of woman who thinks all guys are desperate just move on as I am not.
If you have issues with men and trust just move on I want somebody who is all real and sorted.
If you want a million messages and very guarded about meeting just move on, I want to

meet not a million emails.
If you have younger children or mother living at home move on, I want somebody who is free SORRY but I know what m looking for.
If you think intimacy is a dirty work DEFINATELY MOVE ON.& FAST.
If you can send a decent message with some content Im very happy to reply.
If you don't have a passport move on !!
If you are not comfortable in your own skin and like to look 20 year younger than you really are but everybody knows your old MOVE ON.
If you are in your 50s and wear a mini skirt MOOOOOOVE ON.
If your looking or have enjoyed the attention of younger guys as a Mrs Robinson just move on as I want mature realistic women.

Its ot too much to ask, Im very honest and expect the same, Im very good company and experienced in life having travelled lots, don't take my requirements as an insult but Im not desperate or need and definitely ever waste my time on timewasters. IF your nice get in touch.

REMEBER NO ONE LINE INTRODUCTIOS

AS I WILL DELETE YOU, JUST NEED SME IMAGINATION AND IN RETURN YOU WILL FND A VERY NICE GUY.

Although my fingers itched to message: "Can't spell and grammar terrible... Move on!" I controlled myself, and swiped left.

*

I started to find the age of the swipe quite soul-destroying, questioning the ability to judge someone in less than a second. But, in many cases, there was nothing else to go on; writing anything seemed to have become a bit of a dinosaur. It sat uncomfortably with me that I, too, was now basing my future on a grainy face. Or, even worse, a grainy face covered in flowers, or pretending to be an app-generated dog/cat, etc. It smacked of too much desperation.

So, I went back to the heady delights of profile reading, once more.

13. Catfishing

By now, I was still floundering and swiping on a daily basis, with little or no result. *Can one become addicted to this?* I started to wonder!

I had more or less decided to stop and give my swiping finger a rest, when a very handsome man messaged me. Having read his profile - and admired his abs - I responded.

Conversation seemed to flow and, having covered the basics of jobs, relationship status and children (of which he had none, except for the job part), I asked about his interests. A long list appeared, and I chuckled to myself, as he included being a good lover, along with cooking, reading and online Scrabble. More and more messages arrived, and we moved our conversation onto a messaging site, instead of the dating one. It seemed that perhaps my dreams weren't unreachable, after all, and that maybe, just maybe, I had found someone.

As he was based in Manchester, and I was heading in that direction, in the not-too-distant future, I suggested a meeting, to see how we connected in real life. The response was immediate: he told me that he would love to, but with a big contract coming up, he would need to come back to me with an actual date. No problem. I smiled happily and waited, whilst arranging accommodation for my stay in the city.

The news wasn't great: he apologized profusely, but his contract was due to start, and he was heading to Istanbul for a few weeks, to sort it out. I sighed, but accepted the outcome. Still, we continued to message, for hours at a time. His flight left, though we were still to meet. *What's a few weeks?* I thought.

As the date drew closer to my heading north, I asked when he thought he might be back. Good news for us, he said: he was going to stay and finish the contract, but that would give him enough money to travel with me in the future. *Okay,* I thought, *what's another few weeks?* He then said that it wouldn't be until September. Considering it was still only March, this didn't sit well; I started to wonder if I was prepared to wait that long. I messaged him, explaining that it might be best to leave it, but he could feel free to message me upon his return.

His words changed, turning to messages about how he was falling in love with me, and if I could only wait, it would all come together.

Patience has never been my strong point. Knowing that I couldn't jump on a flight to Turkey, due to work commitments, I began to lose interest.

More and more messages arrived from him, declaring his undying love, and sending picture after picture of himself. Each made him look more and more handsome, and a phrase that my dad had once used started to spring to mind: "Batting above your average." Looking at him, I certainly seemed to be.

Having chatted to family about the situation, one of them, upon seeing the pictures, asked if he was in fact a model. Bells started ringing loudly now, knowing that I wasn't the type a model would usually date. He kept suggesting I check the images he was sending me.

Mr. Handsome actually turned out to be a Canadian B-list actor. Feeling obliged, though not expecting a response, I contacted the actor and told him that his pictures were being used by a "catfish".

But still, I allowed the devil in me to emerge, messaging Mr. Handsome a few more times. By now, he was sending poems and full-blown declarations of love. For a couple of days, I let him.

As I finally pressed "send" on what would be my final message to him, I told him that I was bored of this game now, and asked whether I should call him by his made-up name, or by the Canadian actor's name.

His single word response came back: "O.K."

And, so started a whole new level of online dating: me checking the worldwide web for information on anyone who came into my view, to see if they were real or not.

The devil is in the detail. I should have picked up that he was Turkish, from his cited interest of being a "good lover". *For goodness' sake, woman! You've lived there for long enough, and heard the men say it enough times!*

"Catfish" can be either men or women, who create fake profiles on social networking sites; these predators trick people into thinking that they are someone else entirely. The fabricated life stories and photographs that they cobble together online often contain the experiences, friends, resumés and job titles that they wish were their own, providing a complete window into how these scammers want the world to see them. The emergence of such elaborate social schemes online was brought to light in a shocking way, in the 2010 documentary *Catfish*, in which 28-year-old Nev Schulman fell in love with a gorgeous young woman's Facebook profile, and her voice over the phone, both of which turned out to belong to a middle-aged wife and mother. He had been duped.

I'm still not sure what catfishers get from what they do. I wasn't asked for money, or anything else, which confuses me. The media seems to report many cases of this happening, with a variety of consequences.

For what it's worth, use the web to check everything, before getting involved. Fortunately for me, at least, I only lost hours of time, feeling flattered, rather than losing money, experiencing heartache or much worse. As the saying goes, if it's too good to be true, then it probably isn't.

14. My top ten ways to hook a catfish

1. ***Too good to be true:*** **PHOTOS.**

Do they look like a model? Do they seem way too perfect to be a normal person? Search their photos using Google's reverse search by image; if you find the same images on lots of different sites, linked to different names, or if the images turn up on a stock photo or modelling site, you might want to think twice. *Mr. Catfish* ticked this box extremely well.

2. ***Too good to be true: LIFE.***

Don't be too quick to believe everything you read. If they claim to be a brain surgeon and/or a part-time pilot, who enjoys running monthly marathons and volunteering to save children in Africa, your alarm bells should start ringing.

Thinking back (isn't hindsight a wonderful thing), many of the things he told me were directly linked to *my* life, which now makes me wonder if he actually knew who I was. He couldn't have found anything from my social media platforms, as they are kept private and I manage them very well. Scarily, then, it might have been someone I had already met!

3. ***No photos or webcam.***

Be alert to any profiles which offer no photos. Early in your interaction, ask them to send you a photo and, if they refuse, become suspicious. Having a video/web chat is a great way to explore the level of chemistry between you - if they claim to have no access to a webcam (unusual, these days), your intuition might tell you something.

There was no lack of photographs of Mr. Catfish - in fact, the complete opposite. Just not of himself, as I later found out. His webcam was "broken", hence our inability to Skype.

Silly girl! The klaxon should have been blaring at that!

4. ***Saying exactly what you want to hear.***

Many victims report that the person said all the right things, tapping into their deepest needs, and making only positive comments. In truth, we all know that "real" people have flaws, and tend to say a combination of positive, negative and neutral things, so look out for this.

Their ability to make you feel special is a hard one to walk away from, especially if you're lonely and trusting, as so many of us are. Mr. Catfish talked about his love of travel and history which, for me, was the best type of bait to use.

He also liked playing Scrabble online, and we played many games together. For this, I am actually thankful, as it introduced me to a new way of passing my time; better for me than reading profiles, day in and day out.

5. *Too serious, too soon.*

Real intimacy takes time to build; it is based on trust. If they move too quickly into the realm of love and commitment, try not to be flattered: this may be a sign that they are not legitimate. With the sheer number of declarations of love, and the poems, my man was right up there in that field.

6. *Asking for money.*

This should be a massive red flag (but, unfortunately, many people are still seduced by this)! If they ask you for cash, this is an indicator that their intentions are based on something other than finding love. Walk away! This didn't happen to me, but who can say that it wasn't his intention.

7. *Very low Facebook friend count.*

Check out their Facebook page, as soon as you can. Often, when a catfish sets up his/her false dating profile, they set up corresponding Facebook, Twitter and other social media accounts, to demonstrate "social proof" that they exist. If their other social media profiles appeared online around the same date as their dating profile, this could be an indicator of deception. If their Facebook profile has less than fifty friends, or no people are tagged in their photos, this is also an indicator of a fake profile.

Although I searched, I could find no social media traces of

Mr. Catfish, but then again, I have many legitimate friends who choose not to use these sites, communicating through email. Still, it is worth trying to find them this way.

8. *Traumatic life events.*

Catfish often create elaborate stories, to play on your sympathy, especially leading up to asking for money. Be aware of anyone who talks about major illnesses, traumas or unusual life events, in the context of gaining sympathy. My potential suitor told me he had lost his parents, but that was quite early on in our conversations. Having batted back my own parental experiences, he probably ended up feeling sorry for me!

9. *Excuses, excuses, excuses…*

A key indicator of a catfish is that they will not want to meet you in person (or via webcam). Be aware of anyone who constantly makes excuses about why they can't meet. A good guide is to aim to meet in person, within one month of connecting online.

Mr. Catfish was spot on, and given his sudden departure to another country, with a reasonably convenient excuse, was certainly one to look out for.

10. *Trust your gut.*

Most victims of catfish will report that there were many little signs; lots of occasions when their gut told them "NO", but their heart told them "YES". This is definitely one situation where it is important to listen to your intuition: it's there for a good reason. Your unconscious mind provides hints, when it suspects someone is not the real deal - so, listen to it! For me, in the end, that is what it came down to: my gut. That and my dad's voice of reason in my head.

*

Just as you think it's safe to throw your line out once more, new terms are becoming the norm, in the world of dating.

I always thought "ghosting" was something to do with spirits, haunting you, but it is now a term widely used, to explain when someone suddenly ceases all communication with you. I had that happen a few times!

Then there's "benching", which is when someone you're interested in stops actually hanging out with you, or committing to dates, yet continues to text, tweet or Snapchat you. There was I thinking it was what you do to an injured footballer.

No doubt, there are many more phrases or words out there, or yet to be developed, which will also confound me. Is it my age?

Maybe speed-dating will work for me. Or, should I just head to the nearest Texaco and see what happens?

15. Funny when it happens to someone else!

Feeling that I'm fairly savvy in the pond nowadays, it shocks me when I hear about or read other people's stories.

But, like everything in life, there can be a funny side. This story, printed in a newspaper article, made not only the lady in question laugh, but I suspect many people around the world, too:

> *"A clothes designer, who tried to let a man down gently, following just one date, received a request for cash from him to cover the money he spent on drinks.*
>
> ************, *from London, was only on her second date, after joining the online apps 'Plenty of Fish' and 'Tinder', when a three-year long relationship ended, just before Christmas.*
>
> *Despite the date at a Clapham pub going well, and Miss Brown thinking he was 'normal and sweet', she texted him to let him know she was not interested in meeting a second time.*

However, she was left in disbelief when the man replied to say he was 'devastated' and asked for a 'contribution for the drinks I spent on you', finishing the message with his account number and sort code.

After she had ended up taking his watch home by mistake, the man told her not to post it back because 'it'd be too painful to receive the watch in the post and remind me of you.'

Miss Brown's reply informed the man that she had paid him back £42.50 and donated the same amount again to a donkey sanctuary, claiming she had never laughed so hard.

She said: 'I had only been using dating apps for about a month, mainly Tinder and Plenty of Fish. I met him on Plenty of Fish and I thought he seemed really nice and normal, with a good profession, as I'm a career girl, and he seemed quite sensible.

'I have been a bit of a date monster (before my last relationship), but I'd only been on one other date with someone else before I met him.

'When I got the text, I was crying with laughter - I honestly thought he was joking. But then I realized he was serious.

'Everyone in my office has been snorting

and crying with laughter at the text, too. People have just been like "oh my God, is he joking?" after seeing the message. My life does feel a bit ridiculous at the moment. I just think "why me?"'

In the text, her one-time date expressed his adoration and disappointment at being jilted and admitted he had saved up to take her out. The text read: 'Hi, thanks for your honesty. I had a really nice time with you and the truth is I'm a bit devastated atm (at the moment), having read your note.

'I really fancied you and saved up some money to take you on a nice date; as it didn't work out I'd be grateful if you could send along something to contribute for the drinks I spent on you, thinking I'd at least get to see you again.

'The total cost of the night was £85, and as it'd be too painful to receive the watch in the post and remind me of you, I thought that you might be interested to know the cost of that was €20. Happy for you to do what you feel is right, especially considering my badly damaged feelings atm.'

Miss Brown decided to refund him, but not

without letting him know how funny she found it all.

She said: 'Am a bit surprised - how can he be so devastated about just one date? I only ended up with his watch because we were both messing around and he was wearing my hat, so in return he gave me it to wear.

'When we both went to say goodbye we both forgot I still had his watch on. I decided to pay him the £42.50 back for my share of the cost, but I also donated the same amount to a donkey sanctuary.

'I saw a post on Facebook about them and I think they are such a lovely charity and they post really funny pictures.

'He has since messaged back and he put "I feel like the donkey sanctuary has come out better from this situation." I just text him back saying "Eeyore".'"

16. Huge words of WARNING!

Any dating comes with a risk, whether it be friends helping you to find the man of your dreams, parents arranging a date to help you leave home, or the world of online fishing; it is always advisable to take sensible precautions.

At the start of my online experience, I agreed with my daughter that if I was to arrange a meeting, then the following would happen:

- She would know the place and time of the date, before I left the house;
- I would text on arrival at the meeting point;
- She would message me one hour into the date: a problem at home, which needed my immediate attention, could help me out of a difficult or unwanted date;
- She would phone me after two hours, to double check I was happy; this would give me a second opportunity to do a runner, if necessary;
- I would text her to say I was on my way home.

We have continued this over the years… Well, except for one occasion, when she grounded me for not keeping in touch!

Although having a "get out of jail card" may be overcautious, and someone knowing where I am at all times might seem excessive, nothing is too much, if it keeps you safe.

Through my experiences, I have found that many potential suitors would like my Whatsapp, Hangouts or other contact details, including my phone number. Being a boring old fart, I don't have any of these apps, and being a traveller, I don't have a real phone.

I am anyway very hesitant to share personal information, unless I think there is a chance of something coming of it. I find that once I have told them I don't have any of the relevant apps, and that I would prefer to know more about them before sending any further personal and contact details, it gets rid of them very quickly - perhaps because I don't conform to today's society. Or, just maybe, because they were unscrupulous and wanted my info to scam me, or otherwise. Either way, communication usually stops.

Those which are happy to continue, and who respect my feelings about this, get my full attention… That is, until they disappear, for no known reason!

Looking at it from the other angle, of course: the fact that I have no phone and won't give out any contact details might raise *their* suspicion, and suggest that *I'm* a catfish. Tricky, isn't it?

A recent newspaper article made me glad that I'm as cautious as I am. It told the story of a woman, who met a man for a drink, from an online dating site, and later awoke to find herself being raped. This exposé brought other women into the media, who had also been attacked and beaten, by the same man. His profile claimed that he was a cuddly romantic, who liked cosy nights in; he wanted more than a one-night stand: someone honest, who would not mess him around… He is now serving four-and-a-half years behind bars.

There are, of course, many simple ways to protect ourselves, although I realize that in the heat of the moment of eternal hope, they are easily disregarded.

Make sure you have messaged and received quite a few back, before moving forward. Ask questions which might catch them out: how long they have been single is one of my favourites, and quite often results in lack of an answer - suspicious enough in itself.

Use Skype. It's a wonderful tool, giving you the chance not only to see the person in question, but also to study his or her body language. Look at the background area, when talking online, for tell-tale clues: wives' or husbands' clothing hanging, photographs and the like.

Always meet in a busy place, but not somewhere you usually go - partly to protect your own space, and partly sparing you relentless teasing from your local barman, for the rest of the year! Meet inside the place, and try to get there first, positioning yourself so that you can make eye contact with members of staff, in case you need to summon help.

Let your date leave the venue first and check which way they go. Leave enough time for them to drive/walk a fair distance away, then head in the opposite direction. Sure, it might be out of your way, but your safety comes first. Check your mirror, to make sure they haven't waited to follow you, and go home via a different route. Maybe, make a quick stop on the way, to buy some chocolate, for the rest of the evening! The same applies to those using public transport: get onto a different bus/train, rather than the one you should be using, and get off at the next stop. Yes, it takes longer, but it might keep you safer.

This may all seem over the top, but isn't that better than becoming a media story, after it's all gone wrong?

You also need to balance your approach to online dating. Of course, it is important to have fun, relax, be yourself and enjoy the process, but try to maintain a healthy level of dating skepticism, too. Cast a more objective eye over your own profile and get a friend's opinion. Do you communicate a level of vulnerability or desperation in your profile? I read back through mine, and certainly believe that it is more likely to put any potential menaces off, rather than encourage them… Perhaps, hence the lack of messages!

As online dating becomes more and more prolific, it would seem that the risks get higher, as predators have more platforms to find and terrorize their victims. The only way to fight this is for the victims of these people to report and share their stories - whether they be women or men; each can be equally affected by the deceit, and the physical and emotional abuse which can be inflicted. The more victims step forward, the more the dangerous are dealt with.

Be safe out there.

17. When you're not that into him!

It's bound to happen at some point: you might have met someone, had a few dates and decided that you're not that into them. Or that, having spent some time with them, the boxes you thought they were ticking were actually huge areas of caution and concern. So, you try telling them: *"Sorry – you're really lovely, but it's not going to happen for me."* But, they don't seem to be picking up the subtle hint.

Most suitors will respect your wishes and call it a day, but for some, it might be a problem.

No doubt, if you have had a few dates, or have even started a relationship, you have probably given them access to all of your online platforms. Luckily, if they haven't respected your wishes, and seem persistent in wanting to know the ins and outs of *why* you don't want to see them, or they will just not give up, you have the option to block them.

Personally, I only block people when pushed to the limit. My soft heart will always try to explain, asking them to move on and wishing them well in the process.

In some cases, though, the man seems to have used a harpoon

for his fishing trip, and simply refuses to take his eye off of you, as his catch. This can become scary and stressful, especially when you have used the blocking method on every account you have, and they still seem to get through, sending messages. This starts to form the basis of harassment, and what is more contemporarily known as cyberbullying. I know that these are harsh words to use but, essentially, these are exactly what it is.

The law in the UK states that:

> *"Harassment is when someone behaves in a way which makes you feel distressed, humiliated or threatened. It could be someone you know, like a neighbour or people from your local area, or it could be a stranger, for example, someone on the bus."*

To my mind, someone who refuses to stop messaging you, phoning you or trying to communicate with you causes you distress. It might not be physically threatening, but it can take a toll on your mental health.

The law goes on to state that examples of harassment can include:

- *unwanted phone calls, letters, emails or visits;*
- *abuse and bullying online;*

- *stalking;*
- *verbal abuse and threats;*
- *smashing windows or using dogs to frighten you.*

These are routes which rejected suitors might head down. Being told in a message that you are over-reacting to a situation might seem like a throwaway comment, but it is bullying, and is something that the fishermen and women of the world feel is acceptable to say, to change your mind.

If you are not sure whether you are being harassed or bullied, ask a friend or family member, and watch their reaction – there is your answer.

If so, you can and should take action - that is what the law is there for. It may seem a small and fairly insignificant misdemeanour to you, but it might help to protect someone else in the future. Harassment is both a criminal offence and a civil offence, under the Protection from Harassment Act 1997. This means that someone can be prosecuted in the criminal courts if they harass you. It also means you can take action against that person, in the civil courts.

You might call it dramatic, or over-reaction, but doing so could save your or someone else's life. If nothing else, it might just stop the misery of being continually hounded, in one way or another, by unwanted advances.

18. Cupid's arrow

Having grown bored with fishing, my fingers hurting from too much swiping, a friend of mine suggested yet another online site. By now, I was up for anything, and although my intentions to date were becoming less and less important, it did pass some free hours, looking at the world through rose-tinted glasses.

With a very brief profile, I thought I would allow Cupid to take over. The site's layout was a little different, allowing users to answer hundreds of questions, in our quest to find a match.

By 53 questions in, I was growing bored, and not liking many of them: they seemed very one-dimensional in their context. But, to complete my profile, I persevered.

Finally, with everything uploaded and my computer-generated matches in front of me, I looked at the options on offer. No one grabbed my eye, or my mind. But being by now a veteran, I knew that it takes time.

Within a couple of days, my message inbox was filling rapidly - mostly with American men, who all appeared to be widowed, with children looking for a mom! Fearful from my previous experience of this category of men, I started off in my usual, polite way, messaging my standard *"sorry, not for me"* text.

But, this did not deter them. If anything, it seemed to intensify their liking for me! As the messages escalated, I was continuously reassured that our compatibility wasn't a problem: either the children were at boarding school (something which I would never want for my child), they had a full-time nanny (again, not something I would feel comfortable with), or - and even more alarming to me, as my former teaching brain came out of retirement - that they lived in another country, dependent on and living with a relative. Did these men not know who should be the number-one priority in their world?!

I thought it would help to change my profile details, and ask nicely for men not currently residing in the U.K. to please refrain from messaging me, as well as those who had school-age children or dependent relatives. It didn't. In fact, it failed on all counts, as more and more missives filled my inbox. Well, if they can't take basic directions then they need to keep on swimming; I took great satisfaction in blocking them, one by one.

Still, this didn't seem to make any difference; hundreds more arrived, each day.

Finally, I gave up and closed my account. I went back to my fishing rod, and exercising my swiping finger.

19. From the other point of view

In a bid to fill my evenings, I decided to see what my competition was like. Were other women's profiles so different to mine? Did they say things which actually led to them catching a man, or two?

I changed my search criteria to that of a male and, taking a deep breath, I crossed my fingers that none of the ladies' profiles I was about to read would lead to embarrassing messaging, which might leave me attempting to explain that I was really just being downright nosey.

SALLY

Hi,

Im still to find that special someone. I'm in no rush as I do mean 'special' not just 'someone'. I'm bright and passionate about many things and only hold close others who are genuine and kind with emotional intelligence and integrity. I've a cheeky sense of humour which I like in others too and have a worldly wise view of people, life and myself. I like those who like me aren't afraid to speak their mind and don't suffer fools. I try to look good but I'm not vain and I've achieved successes which I value, even if they are not in the materialistic sense. I'm far from perfect and I'm not looking for that in another either, but a spark and similar values is a must.

I live in a lovely area and enjoy my simple, peaceful homelife which I'm finding more time for. I'm not well off enough to afford fancy trips or holidays which I don't mind, but means I can't offer that or join you on yours- unless your paying:).

Days out, interesting conversation, lazy sundays, cosy nights, cooking & enjoying

meals, occasional boozy nights, talking & listening at the end of a day, socialising together and/or apart while generally caring and looking out for each other while sharing life's ups and downs - I can offer.
If you are not searching for the same; fair enough, let's please not waste each others valuable time so we can find what we do want.
Otherwise, I might hear from you...

Wow, she sounded great! Very honest… well, if you were to believe her!

Maybe I can gain something from this, I pondered. Although, I would hesitate to mention the *"your paying"* part; as long as my date pays his way, I don't have a problem with paying mine.

I considered the next one:

JODIE

Apologies in advance for my opening line, but really, if you might be interested in getting to know me more, then please say more tha "hi" "you look nice", "chat" AND I SAY AGAIN... if I am lucky enough for you to be interested then say something and show me your personality..make an and
Effort!
Really ... having just opened 5 emails - please say more than "hi" !!!
My favourite song is "The Greatest Love of All" and I cry every Christmas when The Sound of Music comes on the TV.
OK, here we go, Well, 5' 8", sociable, funny, blonde, average build, curvy (hope you like curves?), smiley, happy, independent, but like to share.I love to laugh, that's important to me, I can laugh at the silliest of things and want my partner to do the same. I'm tactile and loving, and again looking for the same back. I'm 5' 8" and like to wear heels, so a guy a few inches taller is my preference, (blimey I'm choosy, sorry!).I'm a good listener, an excellent nurse (hee, hee) I love to make my partner feel cared

> *for, loved and happy.I like to go out an do 'stuff' , but I also adore being snuggly with my man (if he's the right one!) on the sofa with a bottle or two of red, just talking, laughing and well, all sorts, into the small hours.Affection is important to me so if you're the type who can't bring yourself to hold my hand in public and kiss me for no apparent reason , whilst I'm cooking or doing mudane things, then you're not for me; I love singing, and I think I'm great at it!!?? my friends probably would disagree, so perhaps you'll hear me one day and then you can let me know you think. So are you, strong, masterful, good looking, sexy, protective, intelligent, articulate and able to make me laugh? Then PLEASE get in touch.I would like to meet a fun, caring, sexy, intelligent and sincere man, to love and laugh with and most of all, be myself with.*

Interesting, I thought. *So, other women are as particular as me?* Another woman who wanted a taller man. I started to feel sorry for the shorter members of the opposite sex.

I read through again, and it dawned on me that she probably received quite a few messages, as her mention of being sexy stood out. Was this the way forward for me? Nope: not my style. Nothing wrong with it for others, just not for me.

LOUISE

Not sure what to say really I'm a genuine, honest very caring person. I love my family & friends more than anything , I enjoy going out having a good laugh & I enjoy cosy nights in watching a good film (i miss cuddling up on the sofa) . I want to meet a genuine, honest man (if there's such a thing), someone who can make me laugh and enjoys family life .... Right let's get down to the nitty gritty because I'm very straight forward & what u see is what u get , I'm not a stick thin women I've got curves (size 14/16) sometimes smaller so if that's a problem please don't waste my time and don't keep asking for me to send pictures, it's boring and if it bothers you don't message me it's as simple as that, all my pictures are recent, so I hope this clears things up !!!!!! Yes there will be prettier, slimmer & younger women on here but no one as nice as me lol :) one last thing I don't do one night stands if that's what your after look elsewhere please :) !!!!!!! Update .... if u want to talk to numerous women on here carry on just don't include me!!!!

And what's with all the bare chest pictures & pictures of what car you own ???

Very feisty, and obviously receiving as many messages as I did, asking for pictures and sex chats. These were always the messages which I chose to ignore, deciding that if they had that little respect for me, then they weren't worthy of my time. My heart felt for her, as her profile concentrated on the frustration of her search. I had to agree with her about the bare chests and the motors. It's a toughie.

*

The more profiles I read, the more I realized that, over the time my rod had been dangling in the water, I had used very similar words in my own profiles. Trying to give an insight, and get someone's heart to flutter, isn't easy for any of us, whichever gender we are.

The pictures varied in content. In contrast to some bloke brandishing his prized fish, women seemed to go more for long-haired cats. Maybe I was missing a trick. Would this enhance my chances? Perhaps a feline could help me catch my very own angel fish?

Did checking out the competition make me feel more reassured, or just sad? It certainly hadn't hurt to look.

So, having copied a couple of lines from one very pretty woman's profile, for possible future use (not entirely sure if that's plagiarism, but doubted she would ever find out), I changed my gender back and continued fishing.

20. Fancy meeting you here

It's bound to happen: when you live in a relatively small area, and a picture pops up of someone you know.

Do you have a sneaky look at their profile and show yourself, or do you just smile wryly and say nothing? Me, being me… well, let's just say that I do things a little differently!

The first time I recognized someone gave me cause for concern: not only was he married, but I knew his wife, through friends - although I knew neither of them well, I was aware that they were definitely a couple. This left me with a dilemma. Not knowing his wife that well, I didn't want to head into stormy waters and tell her, as she might take issue with me; the last thing I needed was a piggy-in-the-middle situation. But, because of my morals, I felt the need to do something; I hate cheaters and liars.

So, taking the bull by the horns – or, perhaps, the dogfish by the hook - I sent him a short message:

"I think you need to either remove your profile or at least tell your wife!" Short and to the point.

He seemed to get the message: his profile disappeared.

I heard a few weeks later that they had just headed off on a second honeymoon. That may be nothing to do with me, but I like to think that perhaps I helped at least one fish swim back to his own part of the pond.

A few weeks later, I spied someone else that I knew, from my local bar. Should I peek at what he had to say, and how he was selling himself, I wondered. But, knowing that he wasn't a dating option for me, I left it alone – yes, *Miss Fussy* again.

A week or so later, I happened to be out for a drink, when who should walk into the bar but that very same man. With the habit of opening my mouth before putting my brain into gear (and I still wonder why I don't get dates!), I smiled and asked how his fishing trip was going. He grinned, offered me a drink, giving me the money to order while he went to toilet, before we sat down to compare experiences.

He told me that he had been online for a quite a few months now, and went on to relate some of his stories:

"I had a message which started *'Hi handsome'*."

Well, you're no Brad Pitt, I thought to myself.

"*Let's go check her out,* I thought. Then, before I had the chance, a second message popped up, asking if I'd like to go to hers now, for sex. I thought on this for a moment, before checking out her picture, and sent my swift reply: *'Thank you for your generous offer, but no thanks. Good luck.'*

"Her reply: *'You sad old tosser!'* She's obviously not great at rejection!!"

I chuckled and thought: *Well, at least you're not just after sex.* I went on to ask what he had thought of her profile.

"Oh, I didn't read that," he responded: "she was a minger!"

I stored thoughts of his shallowness and managed to say nothing; I had no intention of going out with him, anyway.

Following another quick trip to the gents' facilities, he continued with another story:

"I'd seen one with a nice picture and, having read her profile, thought it might be worth a go. Our second message in, she asked me what I enjoyed. I replied, and asked the same question. She responded: *'Money.'* Not going to pay money for it, so I blocked her. Hahaha, hahaha!"

As my drink spluttered across the table, I decided it was time to go; I'd suddenly remembered that I needed to clean the kitchen floor with a toothbrush, or count all the peas in the freezer. I waited for him to return from the facilities once more, before making my excuses and thanking him for the drink.

He smiled happily at me, then came out with: "Shall I come back to yours, then?"

I laughed and said no, before whispering into his ear that it might be a good idea to wipe the white stuff from around his nose.

I left *Mr. Sniffy* to it and wandered home, making a mental note to watch out for the pond weed, which seemed to be clogging up the waters.

21. Hope springs eternal

Just as you're thinking about giving up, something arrives in your inbox, ignites a spark and hope springs eternal, once more.

Mr. Smiley had a lovely profile, which appeared honest, and a grin which lit up the world. Messages sprang back and forth between us for days, as we each found out more about the other, and both admitted that we rather liked each other - daring stuff, in the world of online dating!

Deciding to take the bull by the horns, I messaged, suggesting that we meet up, and was delighted that he agreed. We made arrangements to meet on the following weekend, near to my summer job, and I excitedly started to plan my outfit.

I sent a message on the Thursday, to confirm the time and postcode for the date, and didn't think to worry when I received no reply: we were both busy people, after all. After working the breakfast shift on the Friday, and feeling somewhat deflated by the continued lack of response, I eagerly checked my inbox to see if he had been in touch. He had.

His message explained that he really liked me and thought we had a spark (I sat, happily nodding). He then went on to explain that he had arranged to meet without worrying, as he thought I would cancel prior to the date (I shook my head: why would I cancel?). He then informed me that he actually lived in Holland!

AARRGGHH!! Conned again!

Taking a few moments to compose myself and swallow my disappointment, I wrote back to Mr. Smiley, explaining that he had lied to me and, as discussed in previous communication, that was a total no-no. Therefore, I had no other option but to say goodbye. He wrote back, apologizing, and I smiled sadly, as I blocked him from my account.

As a couple of weeks passed, my thoughts would turn to him, as I went about my job. Then, I had barely been online and had started to enjoy the world, without a swipe in sight, when a new message arrived, from the man himself. He asked how I was and told me that he couldn't stop thinking about me, that he knew he had done wrong and that he didn't expect a response, but just wanted to touch base with me. Okay, I'm a sucker, I admit it, and I messaged back, asking what he expected to happen. He replied that he would do anything.

I pondered this and gave him a chance. I told him that if we could Skype on the following Tuesday, and if he would arrive for a date with me within a month, then I would consider carrying on. I looked forward to the Skype conversation and sent him my contact details, ready for the following day.

Silence. Nothing but silence.

By the Thursday, I knew I had to pull up the big-girl pants and blocked him, once more.

His profile had said that he was a few miles from my locale, and a month or so later, having changed my own area, I spotted his bright smile once more - now claiming to live in Nottingham.

So, you would have thought that I'd learnt my lesson, when Mr. Smiley popped back up again… nine months later. But, it's hard, being attracted to someone and feeling that they might well be a connection… Yes, you've guessed it: I messaged him.

The message was sharp and to the point, detailing that I didn't trust him and that I couldn't be bothered to waste any more time. The resulting answer was sweet, and everything that you could hope for: he missed me; really, really liked me; was scared; and, so on and so forth. A chink appeared in my wooden heart and I once more agreed to Skype.

Now, I know that you're waiting to hear that again it came to nothing. Well, you're wrong! We Skyped and talked - his smile was just as incredible live as in his pictures. The first call lasted for several hours.

After that, messages flew backwards and forwards for days. We Skyped twice a day, and I thought: *Whooppee! This is going to happen!*

Then, of course, he stopped messaging. I know I shouldn't have expected anything else.

After a few days of silence, I sent a message explaining that this wasn't going to work. A week went by, before a communique popped into my mailbox: he'd been in hospital, after falling off of his bike. I felt so guilty for doubting him, and Skyped to see how he was. Bruised and broken ribs were shown off…

We continued to talk to each other, at every free moment we had. Until he stopped again.

Ten days into the silence I knew I had to stop, for my own sanity, if nothing else. I sent my final message and left him to it.

It's not easy, this dating thing.

By this point in my life, I had started to give up on dating, and concentrated on enjoying myself as a singleton.

When, lo and behold, someone new arrived on the scene.

22. Bad breath stops play

My dad always said: "You have to love a tryer."

Having reached the end of a very long day, involving a ten-hour shift on my feet, I flopped down onto a comfy chair, and decided to see how many messages/rebuffs I had received in my absence.

Two messages awaited my attention. The first I quickly disregarded, politely declining his offer to ride him that evening. The second was from a man whose profile appeared to be honest and genuine… Well, as much as one can tell; we all know that isn't much!

The gent in question asked some interesting questions about my travel - another bonus - and seemed forthcoming with information about himself. So, a pattern emerged, of us messaging, for a few hours each day (the number of hours I spend online has to be questioned at times). The conversation flowed and, although a fair distance away, he was happy to travel to my location, to meet up. Smiling, and with a spring in my step, I duly informed my daughter, and we arranged to meet.

I looked forward to the outing. We had organized the meeting at a local place of interest, so I figured that if the company wasn't good, at least I would have something to look at (the cynic in me always rearing its head, when it came to real-life dates).

First meetings are strange. Although he didn't look much like his picture, it wasn't an issue. But, a quick peck on the cheek compelled me to offer him a piece of chewing gum, as we paid for our entrance tickets - it might help! The date passed quickly and he had plenty to talk about, even letting me speak at points, which at least gave me a respite from the breath.

Deciding that I shouldn't be so shallow next time, I agreed to meet him the following day, for a walk and a coffee. His time-keeping was excellent, but the weather was awful, and having walked for several miles, we were soaked to the skin. I suggested a coffee at my work: at least the coffee might mask the halitosis. This would not only allow me the chance to get dry, but, unbeknownst to him, it meant that he would only be alone with me for an hour or so, before my daughter returned from working her shift, so I wouldn't feel any fear or concerns for my safety. Coffee made, we sat and talked. Well, *he* did.

Being me, I had sat in my usual place on the settee, which meant that he sat next to me. The fumes coming from his mouth were toxic, and despite having moved myself to the farthest possible seat, I had my hand over my nose, attempting to reduce the impact as much as I could.

The arrival of my daughter allowed me to jump up and offer her a towel to dry herself, whilst plonking myself down on a nearby chair - clever of me, I thought.

Two hours later, he had yet to pause for breath, and it was

becoming increasingly difficult to hide my yawns. The daughter appeared to have gone into a trance. I waited until he seemed to finish up one of his endless stories, then I leapt in, explaining that I had quite a bit to do and needed to get on with things - nicely wishy-washy, but hopefully a large enough hint. It didn't work.

Another hour passed. I tried to catch daughter's eye, but she appeared to have fallen asleep, sitting upright.

I couldn't take any more, and finally stopped him mid-flow, telling him outright that he needed to go.

"Okay," he said, and carried on talking.

Trying not to scream, I stood up and repeated that he needed to go, this time adding the word: "now". Finally, he got the hint.

He paused at the door, telling me what a lovely time he had had, and asking if we should arrange to meet for lunch tomorrow. With my ears bleeding, and his breath now focused directly on me, I told him I would check my shift rota and message him later.

I left it for a couple of hours, before sending him the nicest message I could, explaining that it wasn't going to happen for me. His response seemed sad and he asked why. Faced with the quandary of what to say, whilst knowing that it would be rude not to respond, I took the coward's way out, going for the "it's not you; it's me" line.

He didn't take the hint and asked for specifics; he left me little to no choice. I tried to phrase the constant talking as nicely as I could, but hesitated over the bad breath. But still, he wanted more.

So, in a final message, I explained that I found his constant barrage of words and bad breath not something I could contemplate. I then became the coward, by refusing to respond to further messages, until I felt the need to block him, when he didn't stop.

I decided it was time to give up on dating. With only days left in the country, I concentrated on packing and saying my farewells to my colleagues and new friends.

23. Turkish delight

I was excited to be in new surroundings, with my daughter and her friend joining me for the first few weeks; I was looking forward to showing someone new around.

With a two-hour transfer, we all logged our devices onto the available wi-fi, to let friends and family know we had arrived safely.

Within moments of an internet connection being made, my swiping app, and that of my daughter's friend, who is also single, started to ping, as messages and likes began appearing. Turning the sound off, I assessed the situation: within ten minutes I had received forty-five likes, six favourites and nineteen messages; boy, did I feel popular? I started to check through them, blocking the *"I want to have sex with you"* and *"we meet tonight?"* requests, whilst swiping "no" for those I didn't like. After half an hour, I couldn't keep up, as more and more flew into my inbox.

I finally turned off the tablet and decided to wait until the morning, when my brain could cope.

The morning sunshine warmed me, as I took a deep breath and turned the technology back on.

Hundreds of messages and likes greeted my eyes.

I started to whittle them down, until I had matched with two men and messaged one; the rest fell by the wayside. Meanwhile, my daughter's friend was still receiving hundreds of messages, many very lurid in detail and questions. She hastily disabled the app.

The one message I sent led to some conversation with a pleasant Turkish man until, not having not seen his height in the profile, I asked the question. You all know by now that I have a thing about height, and his response that he was five-foot-five meant that it wouldn't be happening for me.

Several days passed, and thousands more attempted to contact me, with offers of sex and declarations of love. How anyone could declare love, having seen only a brief profile and a few pictures, was beyond me.

It surely must be time to give it up.

24. Mr. Moneybags

A few days passed and, with the sun shining brightly in the Turkish sky, I sat with my morning coffee, getting my profile fix. I wondered if there were addiction clinics for profile reading! I put in my usual search and smiled at the number of dead fish which greeted me.

I quickly scrolled past the picture of a man holding a whip, before focusing on a smartly-dressed gent, who smiled happily into the distance. One click and I was away. His profile was short and not memorable, but enough to make him sound pleasant. Taking the plunge, I typed in a message and pressed the "send" button.

His response arrived quickly, and we chatted for a while.

He travelled, was five-foot-eleven, had hair, no children and he was breathing... *This might be a goer,* I thought.

The following day, more messages passed back and forth, as I considered how it might be possible to meet. He was aware of my location and, having voiced the question, told me that once he had completed his current contract, he would be free to go wherever he wanted, as long as he could cash his pay-cheque.

"Shouldn't be a problem," I said: *"we do have banks in Turkey."*

"Excellent," he replied, *"would two million be a problem?"*

I choked, before logging off quickly, to give my brain time to work. I must have gone white, as the daughter and her friend rushed to my side, enquiring if I was alright and asking what had happened.

I spluttered out the words: "Two million."

They looked at me strangely. "Two million what?" they chorused.

"Pounds… I think," I whispered.

They looked as shocked as I, as we sat for a few minutes, contemplating the information. I'm not, nor have I ever been money-orientated. I believe in paying my way – and, begrudgingly, that of some of my previous partners, as well – but, keeping up with that amount of spondulicks was way out of my league.

My daughter's friend was the first to recover her verbal reasoning and, having asked for his name and any other information I knew, disappeared into the living room, where her laptop was. Twenty minutes passed, before I heard her calling me.

After settling next to her, on the comfort of the settee, she presented me with a picture. I hummed and hawed; it did look somewhat like him. My response wasn't helpful. She then showed me the delights of LinkedIn, and searched the company name he had given me. It looked fine to me and corroborated what he had said.

She, however, shook her head: "Nope, this isn't right. There is information missing here. It seems fishy to me."

I smiled and tried to look as if I understood the next ten minutes of conversation, whilst she continued to check further details.

In my efforts of trying to obtain further information, I contacted *Mr. Moneybags*, and asked if he fancied a Skype call: at least seeing his face and hearing his voice might be an added bonus, if nothing else. A few minutes later, the wonders of the 21st century enabled us to see each other on screen.

Nervously, I babbled on for a few minutes, trying to assess his character and body language. But, the face on the screen was as static as a picture; he didn't move one inch, in the five minutes of conversation. And, other than saying "hello" and "speak soon", he didn't have very much to say for himself at all – but then, when talking to me, getting a word in edgeways is tricky for anyone!

The call didn't seem to aid my fact-finding mission much, but the daughter's friend was even more adamant that something wasn't right about him. As she worked for a fraud detection department, I took her advice to lose him quickly; with one press of the key Mr. Moneybags was no more.

I considered how many other things I needed to know, before I could be let loose in the world of internet dating. Talk about shark-infested waters!

I deleted the app, much to the delight of my swiping finger, and decided to do the same with my floundering profile. There really didn't seem to be much point in continuing now, considering that I would be travelling around Asia for the next six months. Any dating would have to go on hold.

25. Success at last!

Sometimes, life surprises me.

Having set off on my next travel adventure, I had pretty much put dating, in any way, shape or form, on hold. There was no time to look at profiles, as life itself was far more exciting.

That was until late one evening, as I was trying to cool down in the heat of the Sri Lankan night, when I decided to have a quick look, to occupy my time.

I seemed to have accumulated a huge number of likes, favourites and messages, and a heady hour or so passed, with the feeling of being *Miss Popular*. Having swiped, deleted and considered, I was left with a scant few.

I fired off a couple of messages and looked at the selection of men who had viewed me. It appeared that thousands seemed to have looked, but had made no attempt to woo, message or even favourite me.

At the top of the list was a suave-looking gent. Having glanced at my watch and noted the time, I told myself that I would read his profile and then head to bed:

DANIEL

****

I'm Daniel, single, self employed.. (for 29 years) ...

I have an amazing life, I'm so blessed, I often feel like the happiest man on earth. I'm just missing that special lady to complete it.

Born and bred in England, (mother from India, father English). I'm very lucky to be able to travel a lot. I don't follow any religions, and I don't talk politics..

I have a passion for travel, and exploring other cultures.

I've been self employed for many years. But I have a wonderful team, that allows me, a lot of spare time to travel and enjoy the finer, gentle things that life has to offer.

I would love to find a romantic lady, that loves life, and wants to travel. Someone that believes life is for living, and wants to take sensible, but fun risks to enhance there lives. I love strong, determined women, that go for what they want in life... someone that's not scared to say " I love you "

I've been single for over 6 years now, (out of

choice, to be honest) and feel, now is the right time in my life, to find someone I can love and cherish, and build an amazing future with. I love romance, I love arranging, romantic weekends away, And doing everything in my power, to make the lady in my life, feel loved. I am a true gent, and proud of it. I always treat the lady in my life, like the true princess she is. I'd like to meet someone with grown up children or no young children, someone that's got time to travel, go for nice meals and walks along the beach..

I'm not looking for anything casual. Anyone can get sex, I want to meet someone that I can build an amazing future with.

I have so much love in my heart, I feel now is the right time, in my life, to find someone to share it with.

I'm not into casual dating, or endless "coffee dates", I'd rather wait for someone special to come along.

I have an amazing life, I feel so blessed and so lucky,

I just want to find someone wonderful to share it with Now .

****

Why are women scared to say,
"here's my number, please phone me." ? It's 2018, Not 1918.. Lol.... you are allowed to make the first move..
I'd love to meet a strong lady, that knows what she wants in life, And goes for it .
I'm Not into casual dating or casual sex, I'm looking for a loving long term relationship ..
Distance is no issue to me.. I'd rather spend 5 mins a year with someone I love with all my heart, that lives 10,000 miles away, than spend 24hrs a day with someone I just liked, that lives next door to me..
I never understand why distance is an issue to anyone.. especially when you both live in the same country...
....
Xx

Hmmm, I pondered. A fellow traveller: huge tick; not into casual relationships: another box ticked; and, a man who appeared happy to be romantic, and to look after his "princess": tick-tick-tick! Furthermore, he didn't have a problem with distance: biggest tick yet! My checklist was filling up rapidly. He had hair, his own teeth and was definitely tall enough to measure up to my fussy height criteria.

I sent off a quick line: *"Hi there. Where are you travelling to next?"*

I then shut down my laptop and headed for bed. What would be would be.

The morning brought a reply, and a very interesting response: *"India, in a few weeks' time... And, you? X."*

I grinned to myself and responded: *"Lmao, India, on the 9th. Whereabouts are you going? X."*

Over the next twenty-four hours we established that we would be crossing paths, and that his mother was born in India, as was mine. He had spent six months travelling around Turkey and was looking to move there. With each message, we discovered that we had more and more in common; the smile on my face grew. Could this be fate?

It seemed only sensible for us to arrange to meet, in one of our mutual locations. Having decided on one of the most romantic destinations in the world, we came up with a plan for the Taj.

Have I been lucky enough to find my *sole*-mate, once again, in the strange world of online dating, or might he turn out to be a smelly old trout? Only time will tell.

26. *Keep fishing*

Even with all of its pitfalls and disappointments, maybe the online pool of dating will provide a light at the end of the tunnel, as it has done once in the past.

Don't give up on your dreams, because this medium to help find a partner can work. Hope springs eternal, and I still believe that there is a fish out there for everyone; you just have to catch it, as it swims by. Sometimes it might be a sardine, or sometimes a sprat. But, you never know when the whopper or angel fish will float past… Just, watch out for the sharks!

Safe and happy fishing to you all. x

Plenty of Flounders

ABOUT THE AUTHOR

Jo Roberts is a single parent to a now grown up daughter.

Born in Southport she has lived all over the UK as well as France, Spain and Turkey, she has currently settled in rural Wales and enjoys walking her dog, cooking and visiting places of interest.

A former teacher turned travel blogger and writer she has travelled extensively around the world and enjoys nothing more than meeting new people and learning about different cultures and lives.

ABOUT THE PUBLISHER

L.R. Price Publications is dedicated to publishing books by unknown authors.

We use a mixture of both traditional and modern publishing options to bring our authors' words to the wider world.

We print, publish, distribute and market books in a variety of formats including paper and hard back, e-books, digital audio books and online.

If you're an author interested in getting your book published; or a book retailer interested in selling our books, please contact us.
www.lrpricepublications.com

L.R. Price Publications Ltd.,
27 Old Gloucester Street,
London, WC1N 3AX.
020 3051 9572
publishing@lrprice.com

www.ingramcontent.com/pod-product-compliance
Lightning Source LLC
LaVergne TN
LVHW010622100826
845148LV00014B/3073

9781838061029